5-Minute Stress Relief for Professionals

Clear Mental Obstacles &
Create a High-Performance Mindset

Dan Candell

The Anxiety Relief Guy
www.StressReliefBook.com
www.DanCandell.com

5 Minute Stress Relief for Professionals:
How to Clear Mental Obstacles &
Create a High-Performance Mindset.

By Dan Candell

Copyright © 2023 Dan Candell

ISBN 978-1-7326460-3-2

Dan Candell Group Inc.
300 West Main Street
Northborough, MA. 01532

www.DanCandell.com
www.StressReliefBook.com

Dan Candell is available to speak at your business or conference event on a variety of topics.

Email dancandell@gmail.com for booking information.

What Others Are Saying
about This Book

"We all have different degrees of anxiety during our lives. Some more severe than others. Dan Candell shows you simple and easy techniques and methods to get rid of anxiety in just five minutes! This book is helpful not only to those suffering from anxiety and panic but also to anyone who works with clients that have anxiety and panic. This 5-minute method for anxiety is simple and easy and will change your life quickly and easily and give you the freedom you are worthy and deserving of receiving."—**James M. Vera, author of *The Practical Guide to a Healthy Mind: Proven Techniques to Create the Life YOU Want.***

"Beyond helpful! Candell has produced the easiest, cleanest guide to managing stress and anxiety. He provides the framework, the rationale, and the practical structure for anyone who wants to perform their best, clear the hurdles, and win the race."—**Joseph A. Onesta, clinical hypnosis practitioner, author, speaker, and creator of the Onesta Process.**

"Whether you are a business professional, an entrepreneur, a life coach, or a hypnotist searching for techniques to help yourself or your clients, this is the book for you!

However, before you make any changes, you have to believe you can, and you have to be willing to follow the necessary steps required to make a change. Dan Candell's explanations of stress, worry, and anxiety are the most concise and thorough that I've ever read. There are many exercises to choose from. You can try them as you read or read them all and then choose one or two to practice. Dan not only tells you what to do, he explains what to do step by step. If you are stressed, anxious, or worried, get Dan Candell's book. You will be glad you did!"—**Joann Abrahamsen, certified consulting hypnotist and author of *A Potpourri of Hypnotic Techniques: Adding the WOW Factor to Your Practice.***

"As a colleague, I can honestly say that there is no better person to work with than Dan when it comes to relief from anxiety and stress. His techniques are both out of the box and extraordinarily effective. This book is a must-read for any high-level executive or business professional who has stress in their life… which means it's for all of you."—**Michael DeSchalit, board-certified professional hypnotist and instructor and author of *Unleash the Power of Success.***

Written By a Leading Expert with 20 Years' Experience

Dan Candell is an award-winning ICBCH professional hypnotist and hypnosis instructor, as well as a behavioral communication expert. Dan is an expert at helping people overcome anxiety and mental struggles while helping them achieve a high-performing mindset, both personally and professionally. He is a TEDx speaker, and his TEDx talk has had over ten million views across different social platforms. Dan is also a podcast host and an influencer. He has worked with tens of thousands of people, and his videos get millions of views.

Dan has been a stress and anxiety consultant for companies like Dell Technologies and Amazon. He is known worldwide as "The Anxiety Relief Guy" and specializes in working with business professionals and athletes who experience anxiety, excess stress, overwhelm, and who doubt themselves. He also helps people boost their confidence and their focus and create more of a mental toughness mentality. Dan has also traveled the world, teaching his methods to corporate groups, sales groups, and therapists.

If you would like Dan to speak to your group or work with your team, or if you'd like to join one of his programs, please visit www.DanCandell.com or email Dan at dancandell@gmail.com.

Before You Dive In...

Dan is a content creator and produces helpful podcasts, videos, and posts across many social media platforms. Go to **www.DanCandell.com/FollowMe** or scan the QR code below and follow Dan. Following Dan will give you updates and additional tips, tricks, and techniques to help you reduce stress and anxiety.

If you'd like additional audio and video resources for this book, go to **www.StressReductionBook.com/resources**

Table of Contents

5-Minute Stress Relief for Professionals

Introduction

Do you ever feel like you're on the struggle bus? You know what I'm talking about. You feel stressed out and overwhelmed as the pressures of your personal and professional lives start to collide. On top of that, you may start to worry way too much, and then anxiety hits. You start doubting yourself, and you feel the weight of the world on your shoulders. Even the simplest of tasks start to seem daunting as you try to find some sort of "life balance." You're just trying to manage as everything seems like a challenge, and you're waiting for the other shoe to drop. Because you're feeling this way, it's hard to think clearly, and you're questioning your sanity. One more little challenge can push you over the edge, which becomes the straw that breaks the camel's back…

Welcome to being a business professional, entrepreneur, or business owner.

In today's fast-paced business world, stress has become an all-too-common companion for professionals at all levels. The constant demands of tight deadlines, high expectations, and an ever-increasing workload can take a toll on both our physical and mental well-being. But it doesn't have to be that way. In this book, we will explore various proven techniques and strategies for managing stress in the workplace and show you how to reclaim your sense of control and balance in your professional life. Whether you're a busy executive or a hardworking employee, this book will provide you with the tools you need to reduce stress and improve your overall well-being.

Being a business professional or entrepreneur has a very specific set of struggles that comes with it. It can be like trying to balance while walking on a tightrope. One small thing can cause you to topple over. If your mind isn't in the right place—much like an athlete—you'll be thrown off your game and question yourself and your abilities.

When you're in this mental space, everything can seem like a struggle, and you wonder if you should just give up while you're ahead and be a greeter at Walmart.

Stress is like death and taxes... it's unavoidable. There are small life stressors like losing your car keys and now you're going to be late for a meeting. Then there are bigger stressors like losing a client or account that was worth thousands or millions of dollars to your business. Let's not forget the pressures of deadlines and getting work done on time, having ebbs and flows of income, having teams of people that we have to work with, and anything and everything in between. On top of all of that, you also have a personal life to manage. It's like a constant overflowing cup of yuck.

Up until now, you've probably learned to just live with it. You probably don't know anything different. If you've recognized this as a problem, you may have tried the traditional routes like going to therapy, doing meditation or yoga, or maybe even taking mind-altering medications.

On top of all that, you may have even developed some coping strategies to try and numb or avoid those feelings. These coping mechanisms can include playing too many video games, stress-eating, drinking when you're stressed, stress-shopping, watching too much porn, social media scrolling, playing games on the phone, and any others that you overindulge in to "cope" with the stress that's been weighing you down.

You are undoubtedly already aware of the negative effects stress can have on the body. Stress can be a silent killer that can lead to health complications like high blood pressure, tension headaches, and other aches and pains. It can cause preexisting illnesses like irritable bowel syndrome to get worse. Let's not forget about stress-causing ulcers, tightness in the chest, heart palpitations, and that dreaded eye twitch that just won't go away!

I'm here to tell you that things can and will get better when you dedicate just a few minutes to learning some of these strategies.

In this book, I'm going to teach you several ways that will help you reduce stress and anxiety levels while building resource states so you can "get your head in the game" and function at a better level. Life won't seem like such a struggle anymore.

After reading this book and using the strategies I teach, you'll easily and naturally develop the ability to let stress roll off your shoulders, so the things that used to eat away at you and bother you will no longer do so.

Just by making a few small adjustments and doing some of the strategies and concepts that I will teach you in this book, you'll feel less stressed, calmer, more in control, and even more clear. Each strategy I teach will take less than five minutes to implement, and most people start noticing themselves feeling better immediately. These small five-minute strategies will have a major and often life-changing impact. I'm excited for you. I know these will work for you as they have worked for hundreds of thousands of people that have applied these same strategies from watching my videos, listening to my podcast, working with me in my group programs, or even after becoming my private clients.

Background

I was 22 years old and had just graduated from college when I began my first clinical hypnotherapy practice. I started taking on any and every client I could. I wanted to get experience working with a wide variety of issues. I was also on a quest to figure out who and what I really enjoyed working with. I worked on nearly every problem imaginable. My initial goal was to see four clients per week. My first several clients came in with stress, anxiety, worries, and fears. I would help people over two to four sessions and teach them the skills necessary to eliminate fears rapidly, reduce their stress, and even eliminate chronic anxiety, worries, and doubts.

I also worked with people who had the "typical" issues that the average hypnotist would help resolve. I assisted people in stopping smoking, losing weight, stopping biting their nails, and stopping other bad habits. I also helped athletes with their performance, helped resolve fears and phobias, helped people resolve sexual dysfunctions, and worked with people with ADHD to help them focus and concentrate better, etc. I even used hypnosis in a lot of very interesting ways as well. I worked with witnesses of crimes to recall certain details of the crime (ranging from murder investigations to petty theft), as well as working with people who believed they were abducted by aliens. I was kept on my toes working with a wide variety of people and issues. I worked with kids, teens, and adults of all ages. However, my results would vary.

Many people would get really good results, but others would get subpar results at best. I started to look into why people weren't getting results, and I became aware that a traditional hypnosis approach wouldn't always do the trick, just like most people going to traditional talk therapy wouldn't always do the trick either.

That realization led me on a quest to research and learn everything I could about different therapeutic modalities. I started learning about cognitive behavioral therapy, dialectical behavioral therapy, acceptance commitment therapy, psychosensory therapies, energy psychology, energy healing, and much more. I even researched the psychology of voodoo and spellcasting at one point (that got weird really fast!).

I started noticing trends. Each modality had some parts that made it very effective. It was then that I realized focusing on just one approach wouldn't cut it. I took the most successful elements from all these therapies and modalities that I learned and combined them into an integrated approach.

I began using this unique blend of methods from various disciplines, and it started resolving really deep issues that people had. I called this unique blended approach my *rapid relief resolution model*, which later developed into *rapid relief transformation for business professionals.*

The work I was doing with people spread like wildfire, and my waiting list grew. People were flying across the country to come to my office so I could do an accelerated program with them, and they loved it. But I just didn't have enough time in the day to see all the people who needed or wanted to work with me. To help with the high demand of my ever-growing client list and the rapid increase in stress and anxiety levels, I began creating digital programs and transitioned to seeing people in groups.

Word spread even more, and I started traveling internationally and working with executive teams from companies like Dell Technologies, Amazon, and many others. I'm happy that my approaches to stress and anxiety relief are now being used by tens of thousands of people around the world. I feel honored and blessed that people are using my strategies to create breakthroughs in their lives as they apply these simple strategies to experience more peace, more self-control, and more confidence and freedom in their careers, their businesses, and their personal lives.

I'm confident that you will also create some of these same results in your life when you apply the strategies I teach in this book.

Why Business Professionals?

I often get asked, "Why do you work mostly with business professionals when everyone can benefit from your methods?"

Here's why…

When I worked with people through certain challenges and struggles, I noticed that business professionals, business owners, sales professionals, entrepreneurs, CEOs, executives, etc., seemed to benefit the most from my approach. They follow my program and take action on what I teach them because they have more to lose if they don't. Most professionals have people who rely on them not only personally but professionally as well. If they're stressed or anxious in their personal life or experiencing a challenge, it carries over professionally as well. And when they're stressed or anxious in their professional life, they often carry it into their personal life too.

In the business world, stress is a common experience for professionals at all levels. Numerous factors, such as tight deadlines, heavy workloads, financial constraints, and uncertainty, might contribute to it. Stress can also be caused by interpersonal conflicts or problems, such as difficult relationships with colleagues or supervisors.

The effects of stress on business professionals can be significant. In the short term, stress can lead to decreased productivity and effectiveness, as well as physical and emotional health problems. In the long term, chronic stress can lead to more serious health issues, such as heart disease and depression. Stress can also take a toll on personal relationships and lead to burnout, which can result in an employee leaving the organization.

When someone in business gets stressed, worried, anxious, or overwhelmed, that's when doubt creeps in, and they start to get frustrated with themselves because they aren't functioning at the high level at which they should be functioning.

When we as business people get stressed, I can guarantee that you're not the only one who notices. Stress throws off your mood; you start to spiral, and you may even have a short fuse with people around you. Other people start avoiding you, and you start avoiding situations where you anticipate feeling stressed or anxious.

I often get asked to work with sales and executive teams to help decrease stress and doubt and increase confidence and determination so they can close higher sales numbers or reach out to more prospects. However, there was one team that I remember working with in some type of financial sales division. This team wasn't bringing in the number of leads or sales that they were expected to. The problem was that two team members confessed to me that they were so scared to talk to people that they were faking making calls. Obviously, that wasn't a good situation, and it wouldn't be long before their lead found out. After working with them for about an hour, they made more calls. They quickly climbed to be the top performers on their team because I taught them how to control their emotions, reduce their performance anxiety issues, and trust in themselves to make meaningful connections with people and solve problems.

From one business person to another, I know you'll use what I teach you in this book, and you'll be able to apply it to both your personal and your professional life.

How to Use This Book

Within the context of this book, I share many insights into stress and anxiety in relation to being in the business world. This can help you whether you are a business owner/entrepreneur, sales professional, CEO, executive, or work for a company or organization. I share with you many helpful strategies, techniques, and insights that I have shared with many of my one-on-one clients.

To get the message across, I also share a lot of examples and stories from my clients— both individual clients and clients who are in my group programs.

When you're going through the book, it will be helpful for you to set aside time to practice some of the strategies I'm talking about. Some require you to take out a piece of paper and write something down; others are more thought exercises.

When you do the thought and mental reprogramming exercises, I recommend that you don't just wait until you're stressed or anxious to use them. Practice them when you're not stressed out as well. You'll learn them more easily if you build them into your day. I recommend setting aside three minutes three times a day to practice one of these exercises.

I include a variety of exercises because some may work better for some people and some situations, whereas other exercises may be more effective for others.

Practice all of them and experiment. See which ones work best for you. Also, take time with them. If you don't get immediate results, don't get discouraged. Come back to them at a later time if you need to when you can be fully present, and you'll be more likely to get better results when you use them.

The point is to use them until they become second nature. The more you use the strategies in this book, the better they'll work. The better they work, the less you'll have to use them because you'll naturally start to feel better. I have also prepared a resource guide to help you through some exercises, you can access this by going to www.StressReliefBook.com.

Chapter 1:

A Crash Course on Stress and Anxiety

After working with tens of thousands of people worldwide who have various problems, I've seen a reoccurring theme in every client. They have some level of stress and anxiety that contributes to their problems. If I could help people with one thing, it would be to help them control their stress and anxiety levels so they feel more calm, confident, and in control. Learning how to control your stress will also lead to the ability to control any uncomfortable feelings or emotions.

For many people, stress has become a consistent theme in their lives, and they just get used to it. Stress then starts spilling over into all areas of their lives. It can cause sleepless nights, irritability, mental fog, and the inability to think clearly and get things done. Persistent stress is like a constant overflowing cup you're carrying around with you and will start to spill into other areas of your life if not remedied.

A good way to understand stress or anxiety is by thinking about it like an oversensitive alarm. Think of a smoke detector that you have in your house. If there's a fire and the house fills with smoke, you want the alarm to go off, and that's where it becomes useful. It alerts you that there is danger and to take action, which is an appropriate response. But when the alarm sounds if you turn on your stove or put toast in the toaster, it's too sensitive and starts alerting you at times when it doesn't need to alert you. Stress works in the same way. We don't want it to go away 100 percent because then we wouldn't be aware of any threats. But when it starts affecting you negatively and going off all the time, it's no longer useful. It can be a constant annoyance and something you just learn to live with instead of controlling it.

My goal throughout this book is to help you rewire your internal stress alarm. This will be accomplished in two ways:

1. By shifting your perspective about the causes of stress.

2. By controlling your stress responses so the things that used to bother you don't bother you anymore.

No one is exempt from feeling stressed or anxious. You could be the CEO or president of a multi-million-dollar corporation, you could be a business owner, or you could be a nine-to-five employee or a private contractor, and stress can still sneak its way into your life.

I attended a massive marketing conference in September 2022 that drew over 5,000 people. The keynote speaker was Marcus Lemonis from the television program *The Profit*. He came on stage and, within ten minutes, disclosed his battle with his own mental health struggles—most of his struggles stemming from stress and anxiety. This goes to show you that stress and anxiety can be something that can show up for anyone at any time.

I am writing this book from the perspective of a business owner for other business professionals.

Let's face it… being overly stressed and anxious literally makes us stupid. The more stressed we are, the more cluttered our mind is, making it difficult to think clearly. When we're stressed, the simplest task can become a major chore.

In the next couple of chapters, I'm going to help you understand your stress better. You're going to understand the sources and how they work in your mind and body. When you understand it more, you can start changing your stress responses. In the chapters to follow, I'm also going to give you some of the exact strategies that I use with people in my VIP programs so that you can begin changing your stress response.

Client Example: Several years ago, a client came in and reported severe tension headaches. It was affecting his sleep and his ability to focus and make decisions. He was the CEO of a major franchise, and he was constantly on high alert, worrying about what problems he'd have to face each day. Of course, this was causing him a great deal of stress. He asked me if I could teach him pain control so he could reduce the pain of the headaches and function better.

I told him, "No. No amount of pain control will solve the problem long term."

I explained that the pain he was feeling was just a symptom of being so stressed out and on high alert all the time. Just in case (I always have to play it safe), I had him get checked out by a doctor just to make sure there were no underlying or preexisting conditions that would cause a headache.

Once he got a clean bill of health, I worked with him over the course of about three or four sessions, and within just a couple of weeks, his headaches went away, he was sleeping better, and (here's a bonus), his younger son stopped having temper tantrums.

I know that seems far-fetched, but good ole Dad was putting so much focus on the business problems that he had been carrying the stress home with him, and his son would notice. When Dad gets stressed, he often has a short fuse and loses his temper. The son learned to model his dad's behavior and started throwing temper tantrums not only because that's what he saw his dad do but also because it got him attention from his dad. When his dad started controlling his stress levels, he was more present and pleasant with his son and gave him positive attention instead of feeding into the stress-induced temper tantrums.

Chapter 2:

What Is Stress, REALLY?

Stress is a natural response to demanding situations or challenges. It's the body's way of preparing for action and is characterized by physical, emotional, and mental changes. When faced with a stressor, the body's "fight or flight" response is activated, releasing hormones such as adrenaline and cortisol, which can increase heart rate, blood pressure, and blood sugar levels, among other things.

Stress is a subconscious response. The more you get stressed and anxious, the easier it is to get stressed and anxious again. This is due to neuroplasticity and what is called *Hebb's Law*. This states that neurons that fire together wire together. The more you repeat something, the easier and more natural it becomes. Think about the first time you drove. It was a very conscious process. You had to think about your hands and their position on the steering wheel. You had to think about the amount of pressure you applied to the gas pedal and the brake pedal, and it was all very mechanical. But after you learned how to drive, it became a subconscious activity and required less of a conscious thought process.

Stress and anxiety happen in the same way. It's a patterned response. After you feel stressed out a few times, you begin perceiving all situations that are similar as stressful as well. Stress is merely a reaction to a perceived threat.

The interesting thing is that our subconscious mind cannot distinguish a real threat from an imagined threat; it reacts just the same to both. When you learn how to control the stress response by changing the way you think and then stopping the natural bodily stress responses, you'll be one of those people who will be able to hold their own no matter how difficult or trying things may be.

Chapter 3:

The Anxious Truth

There are many myths and misconceptions about stress and anxiety. Most of those untruths come from a broken and outdated therapeutic model. These falsehoods make people believe that they are broken beyond repair or that it will take a long time to get better. Many people are also taught that medication is the only thing that will make things better. These are all things that are lies that we're being fed, and they can leave people feeling hopeless.

Here are some of the most common misconceptions:

Stress & Anxiety Is a Disease or a Mental Illness

Quite often, when it comes to stress and anxiety, you hear the words "disease" or "disorder" thrown in there. Panic disorder, post-traumatic stress disorder, general anxiety disorder, and social anxiety disorder. It's important to know that these are *just* labels. Sometimes people like labels and live by those labels. Feeling stressed, worried, anxious, overwhelmed, etc., does not mean you are mentally ill, and it does not mean you have a disease.

I have a lot of people that follow me on TikTok, Instagram, YouTube, and Facebook. On these platforms, I posted a video that was meant to be helpful and reassuring. It was something to the effect of, "If you're struggling with stress or anxiety, it doesn't mean you're mentally ill, and it doesn't mean you're weak, and it doesn't mean that something is wrong with you. Many people that I know who are struggling with anxiety are actually some of the strongest individuals I know because they feel fear, they feel challenged, and they still live their life."

Of course, there were a lot of supportive comments, but there were also a lot of people coming at me saying, "You're wrong. You don't know what you're talking about. Anxiety is a mental disorder, and it's a horrible disease!"

People got angry that I was telling the truth and that nothing was wrong with them. But why did they get angry?

Some people like to think that something is wrong with them because it gives them a sense of peace, knowing that they have a reason for how they feel and that it's not all coming from the inside. Struggling with stress and anxiety is not your fault, so there has to be something else to blame. When people experience trauma or are in a toxic workplace, relationship, or family, they often build a level of resentment that they have to put time and often money and resources into getting help. So they unconsciously want to live in the confines of their "illness" because it removes some sense of responsibility from the person who is struggling.

Anxiety and Stress Are Genetic

When people initially become my clients, I frequently hear, "My whole family is anxious; it runs in our family." There's no proof or concrete evidence that anxiety is genetic. Anxiety and stress responses are learned, and they become conditioned in us. I'll explain in the next couple of chapters how this happens.

It Will Take Years of Therapy to Overcome Stress and Anxiety

This is a myth that grinds my gears. First, I am a fan of therapy and counseling. It can help people process their way through life challenges, relationship issues, tragedies, etc. But... if you've been going to therapy for years for the same problem, it's time to switch methods. Since stress and anxiety responses are conditioned into us, when you know how, you can unlearn those responses. In this book, I will show you several ways that you can start rewiring your mind.

You Have to Know the Cause of the Stress or Anxiety

The more we go looking for problems, the more problems we find. You don't have to know the exact cause of your stress or anxiety to resolve it.

Stress Only Affects Weak People

This is untrue. As I shared previously, celebrities, parents, business owners, and people who are extremely intelligent and mentally strong can still struggle with stress and anxiety.

Stress Can Be Resolved by Focusing on God, Doing Yoga, Breathing Exercises, or Going to the Gym

These things can help a person deal with certain feelings, but they won't solve the problem. For most, anxiety and stress become problems that occur in the mind and then trigger physical responses. Then we can become oversensitized, and we start feeling the stress in our bodies before we realize what we are thinking.

People Get Stressed & Anxious Because They Want Attention & to Create Drama

Many of my clients who were feeling overly stressed or anxious were often criticized by friends, family, or co-workers who thought that they were overexaggerating or overly sensitive. They would be told things like, "Stop being so dramatic" or "Just don't let it bother you and move on with your life."

Everyone would do that if it were that simple, but when you learn techniques that can boost your confidence, self-control, and tranquility, the people who used to be critical of you will start to marvel at how you are handling things so well!

Avoiding Stress Will Make It Go Away

It's natural to think avoiding stress and anxiety will make them go away. It doesn't. It makes it worse. Many of my clients tell me, "I keep trying to stop myself from thinking about ......" (whatever thought they're trying to avoid).

I caution my clients when they do this. Every time you try to avoid stress or tell yourself, "I can't feel like this anymore. I need to stop feeling like this," your subconscious mind raises a red flag in that thought and keeps revisiting it to figure out why you don't want to think or feel this way anymore.

Instead of trying to avoid it or telling yourself that you have to stop feeling anxious or stop worrying, reassure yourself that this is only temporary and you're going to shift into a better way of handling what's going on.

Chapter 4:

Types of Stress and Anxiety

There are many types of stress and anxiety. Some people feel stressed or anxious only when there is a certain type of trigger or situation. This is the case with social anxiety, performance anxiety, or even making calls or speaking in meetings. Other people feel that there's an undertone of stress and anxiety that's always there and may never go away. Anxiety becomes part of their personality because it's usually a learned response when they're very young.

It could also result from trauma or growing up in a chaotic household. This frequently results in hopelessness or makes the person have a generally negative outlook on life. I'm going to list a few categories of stress and anxiety, and you may fit into one of many of these categories.

Situational Stress

Situational stress is where a lot of stress starts for people. This type of stress is usually short-term and the result of a situation, event, or specific time. Situational stress is something that affects us all, whether it's while studying for an important exam or during a business presentation. It can seriously impair our capacity for immediate concentration and clear thinking, often leaving us feeling overwhelmed and unable to make good decisions. In some cases, situational stress may even lead to panic attacks, physical symptoms like sweating and shaking, and depression when faced with a concerning situation. Fortunately, with the right strategies, situational stress can be managed effectively or avoided altogether by learning how to calm your stress response and create a problem-solving mentality. I will share some of these strategies later in this book.

Specific Stressors and Anxieties

For many people, there are specific triggers that bring on a stress response. They can be supervisors, specific employees, or anything that can be difficult to deal with. This is where stress is a little different from anxiety. A perceived threat or challenge, such as a tight deadline or a challenging conversation, can cause stress which is a common physical and psychological reaction. Stress can spur us on to take action and help us work through issues; therefore, it can be beneficial in small doses. But chronic stress or stress that is recurring is unhealthy.

Anxiety, on the other hand, is an emotional state characterized by feelings of worry, nervousness, and unease. Unlike stress, which is typically triggered by a specific event, anxiety is often more chronic and can be triggered by a variety of things or nothing at all.

Anxiety can linger in the background. It is usually connected to the anticipation about feeling anxious. Anxiety can be characterized by feelings of worry, nervousness, and unease.

Many anxieties operate this way. Let's look at social anxiety, for example. This anxiety usually happens long before the social event or meeting actually happens. Many people with social anxiety will start to feel anxious when they first find out that they have to attend a social or business gathering, and just the mere thought of it will cause minor panic. For many, leading up to the event, the feeling of anxiety will get worse, and then they find ways to avoid the thing that was making them feel anxious.

Compound Stress

If you experience a number of challenges over a relatively short period of time, your mind begins to anticipate that bad things will happen. Your mind always wants to keep you prepared so that it can keep you on high alert. Even when things calm down around you, you may still feel like you're walking on eggshells or like you're waiting for the next shoe to drop. It's almost as if you feel like you're always bracing for impact. Many people also consider this to be a form of PTSD.

Client Example: A very nice man who was in his early fifties found his way into my program. He owned several coffee shop franchises and achieved great success from his forties on. He sought out my help when his anxiety was becoming difficult to manage, and it wasn't as easy to hide from his family or his employees anymore. People started to notice something was off.

When I asked him to pinpoint an instance that may have caused him anxiety, he was unable to precisely identify it. When people first join my program, I have them go through an *anxiety audit*. I ask them to describe any life challenges that may have happened within a certain period of time. Usually, they rattle off five or six difficulties that they had within a year of the anxiety starting to gain momentum, and at first, they don't see the correlation.

It was the same with this client. He told me that over the past two years, his main residence was ruined in a hurricane, his wife was diagnosed with uterine cancer and needed a hysterectomy, his dog died, and his kids moved off to college. That's a lot to happen in two years. All those events were stressful, and it was just too much for him to handle. As a result, his mind began anticipating that more and more bad things were going to happen. The good news is that we were able to resolve and reduce his stress by communicating a message to his subconscious mind that all that stuff was in the past and he didn't have to always be on edge.

Chapter 5:

Lifelong Stress and Anxiety Resulting from Trauma

This category deserves its own chapter and its own book altogether. One of my next books will be about resolving trauma responses.

Many of our problems today stem from our experiences as children. **We are trying to solve problems now the same way we did when we were younger.** Chances are, it didn't *really* work then, and it isn't going to work now.

Many professionals I work with have anxiety and stress that they can trace all the way back to when they were younger. This is often the result of trauma, family problems, or abuse. However, it doesn't always have to be a trauma that happened throughout childhood. It can even be a toxic or abusive relationship, a toxic work environment, or seeing a family member die.

When a person experiences trauma earlier in life, it can affect how they live their life, work, and run their business. Living through trauma teaches us a set of coping skills that we repeat in adulthood. For most, these coping skills can lead to difficulties in their personal and professional life.

One of these possible coping skills is chronic people-pleasing. This is characteristic of growing up in an abusive household or growing up where alcohol or drug abuse was prevalent. When we're younger, we learn ways that we think are problem-solving strategies. What they're really doing is just keeping the peace to avoid being abandoned. We often go into *please and appease* mode to avoid conflict and confrontation because we learn early on that conflict and confrontation do not lead to anything good.

I've also worked with many individuals who started getting anxious at certain times of the day or around certain people. There was one particular client I remember who said she often gets anxious at around 6 p.m., but it mostly happens on weekdays. When we traced that feeling back to its origin, we discovered that was the time she had to be anxious because that's when Dad came home, and Dad took out his frustrations on his entire family, so the defense mechanism was to avoid Dad at all costs and to walk on eggshells when she was around him. Another defense mechanism she used was to fear men that she perceived were in positions of power.

There are four main switches that can trigger a trauma response or cause us to be more sensitive and receptive. When you're aware of what these four switches are, it will help you understand why you are the way you are and what may have influenced certain facets of your mental programming.

The first switch is age. Up until the age of seven or eight, we're in a constant state of heightened suggestibility. We don't really judge what we're being told, and we accept most of what we're taught or told as having to be true. If something traumatic happens here, our little impressionable minds will soak it up, record it, and keep playing back those emotions or patterns. When something traumatic or difficult happens as children, we don't have the mental capacity or know-how to handle it, yet many of us were put in situations as children that most adults would have a hard time dealing with.

The second switch is trust, authority, and credibility. When someone we trust or look up to tells us something, we don't really judge it. We often accept it as fact. Think about it. When you go into the doctor's office, you're going to do what the doctor says, and you're not really going to question them. When you're young, you're taught to listen to and obey people older than you. If a parent or teacher tells you something or, worse, does something to you, it's going to have more weight in your mind, and it will become part of your programming. This is also true if we see someone we trust or respect behaving or acting in a certain way. We want to model people we respect, so we behave as they do.

I remember working with a very young girl. She was seven years old and had a debilitating fear of spiders. I asked her where she learned to be afraid of spiders, and she said clear as day, "My older sister! She's four years older, and I want to be just like her. When she walked upstairs last summer, she started screaming and yelling because she saw a spider." BINGO! We talked for about five more minutes, and then I did a technique called the fast fear release.

About ten minutes later, we went outside, where I knew there would be spiders crawling around, and she pointed at the spiders and said, "Look! How cool! They're spinning webs! They're so pretty!"

The third switch is heightened emotion. Whenever you experience a heightened emotion, either good or bad, you're more open and accepting of new ideas. Chances are, when you acquired some of these defense mechanisms, it was during a time when you were sad, scared, upset, etc. These are all emotions that will bypass our judgment, and a program can sneak right into our minds.

The fourth switch is repetition. You may have heard that repetition is the mother of learning. This is true. The more we do something, the easier it is to do and the more natural it becomes. Chances are, you repeated an anxious or stress response so much that it became your natural way of being. On the converse, you probably don't repeat relaxation or calm responses very much, so it makes sense that it may be harder (at first) to let yourself relax.

My dad was always a pretty anxious guy. He had a very difficult upbringing, so I can see why he was like that. Unfortunately, he didn't realize that there was a better and healthier way of life until the end of his life. My dad and I were best friends, and he always treated me with respect, love, and compassion. Drug and alcohol abuse was a theme in my family, so my dad and I would often talk about the challenges and struggles we both went through when we were younger. However, I had a much different perspective than my dad did. He would always question how I developed my "Go with the flow. It's no big deal" mindset. Many of my friends say the same thing about me. They say, "Dan, we don't know how you've dealt with the things you've had to deal with in life, and you're the most functioning one in your family. How are you not in a straitjacket in a room with padded walls?" Then we all laugh.

Here's how I can be more Zen and go with the flow. First, I trust myself. I trust in my abilities to be okay. Second, where most people practice and repeat stress and anxiety responses, I practice and repeat calm and relaxation responses several times a day. Whenever I work with a client or a group, I go through the same relaxation and calming exercises they do. So now I naturally can feel calmer and more relaxed instead of stressed and anxious.

I'm NOT saying I don't get stressed. I do. But even then, my stress level is pretty minor compared to what it could be.

In this book, I will teach you how to do the same thing. I will teach you how to practice being more calm and relaxed and in control, so *that* becomes more of your default conditioned response.

Chapter 6:

Shifting Your Perspective

It's so easy to get so clouded in the stress fog, and when we're there, getting out of that can seem impossible. While we're in this fog, we forget that we have choices, we forget about boundaries, and everything seems like such a struggle.

When this happens, we need a wake-up call. This wake-up call can be the lightbulb moment that shifts our perspective and can open us up to getting that *mindset reset* we desperately need. In this chapter, I'm going to share a case study with you from one of my former clients that will also teach you a mindset hack you can use to shift your perspective and help you realize you have choices that you may not be seeing because of the stress fog that's keeping you trapped.

It was 2015. My office phone rang, and when I answered, a woman on the other end frantically began telling me her story. She was 45 years old and was a very well-known realtor in some of the surrounding towns. To her clients, she seemed confident, calm, cool, and collected. But on the inside, she was a wreck. She was so overwhelmed with everything she had to do she'd started doubting herself about the listing prices that she would set for the houses, and what's worse, she was completely disconnected from her husband and her two kids.

Her kids would say things like, "Mom, when will you have time for us?"

Her husband would say things like, "Michelle, I don't even know who you are anymore. You're always so stressed out it's impossible to talk to you."

As a consequence of being like this for so long, she'd get angry at herself for letting these things get to her, and then she'd often lose her temper around her family.

I agreed to work with her because she was about to give up. She was about to hang up her hat as a realtor, and she was afraid that her husband was going to demand a divorce.

It's safe to say that stress was taking over her career, her personal life, and her relationship. She wasn't sleeping well. She'd have these mental and emotional breakdowns, and she'd get into constant arguments with her husband and her two kids. She started resenting herself and started hating her position as a high-powered realtor.

After hearing this, you may think Michelle's story sounds vaguely familiar. This is the story of so many people, whether they own their own business, work for a company, or are top-level executives.

Here's the question you may be asking yourself. Did Michelle ever get relief? Here's what happened...

I agreed to take Michelle on as a client. She showed up for the first session, and I taught her two very simple ways to take the edge off. I taught her two strategies that I will teach you in the future chapters of this book.

Within the first half hour of the session, after doing some inner work with her, she noticed that she was already feeling lighter and more optimistic.

Then I told her, "Okay, Michelle, for these inner changes to last, you have to make some outer changes and start setting some very small boundaries."

One boundary I asked her to set for herself and her family was to not answer business calls after 7 p.m. I even wrote out an outgoing message that she could record as her voicemail prompt: "Hi, you've reached Michelle of XYZ Realty. Between the hours of 7 p.m. and 7 a.m. I take family time. Please leave a message, and I will get back to you promptly in the morning. For more urgent matters, please text my assistant at ...."

Just when I thought everything was going well, Michelle heard that and rolled her eyes so high in her head I thought they were going to fall out of her face holes. Then she glared at me, looking at me like I had eight heads, and said, "ARE YOU CRAZY? I CAN'T DO THAT!"

I said, "Okay, Michelle. Tell me all the other things you 'CAN'T' do."

Here are some of the things she rattled off.

> "I can't respond to people right away and I have to make people wait."
> "I can't spend more time with my kids."
> "I can't return all my emails."
> "I can't have my assistant take on more responsibilities."
> "I can't finish painting my bedroom."
> "I can't sit down and have dinner with my family."

The list went on of everything she told herself and even *convinced* herself that she "can't" do...

I had to get Michelle to shift her perspective, and I had to get her to do it quickly because I had to get her to realize what she was doing. She was lacking willingness. She had to be willing to make some small adjustments so she could get big results.

I said to Michelle, "Okay, I see all the things you tell yourself you CAN'T do. Let's change one thing. Let's change the word 'can't' to 'won't' or 'choose not to' and see how *that* feels different."

I had her repeat everything she told me but put in the words "I choose not to" instead. It became:

> "I choose not to return all my emails."
> "I choose not to spend time with my kids."
> "I choose not to have dinner with my family."
> "I choose not to set time aside for my family."

I explained to her these are all choices, and by choosing *not* to take responsibility to change these things, you're choosing to keep the stress on you and in your life, and you are choosing to suffer the consequences.

After this exercise, Michelle agreed to start small by recording that outgoing voice message.

Now, back to you in the studio.

Stress, anxiety, overwhelm, doubt, worry, and all the other manifestations of those feelings can cloud your judgment and even make you believe some things about yourself that aren't true. Stress and anxiety can make you think that you're powerless or that you don't have options or choices. Often when we're stressed, we can't see the solutions, no matter how obvious they may be. Even when people point out some of those solutions to us, we often deny that they can solve our problems.

Here are some key points when reducing your stress levels:

1. Willingness: You must be willing to change and shift your perspective. But start small. It can start with a boundary, and it can start with a conversation; it can start by setting an auto-reply message. You also have to be willing to use different approaches, even if they seem difficult at first.

2. Trust: You must trust the process, and you must trust yourself. Stress can trick you into not believing in yourself.

3. Intention: Whatever changes you're making, set the intention that "This is to help me feel better and help my life get easier and more enjoyable."

4. Belief: You must believe that what you want to achieve is possible for you, and you must

believe that you can be the person you need to be, even if you don't know how.

Here is a very simple exercise to convince yourself that it's time for a change and that stress is costing you health, wealth, and happiness.

Just like with the story of Michelle, I had her list down all her perceived limitations in the form of "I CAN'T."

Step 1. Take a few minutes to write down all your "I CAN'TS."

Step 2. Look at all your "I CAN'TS" and let yourself notice what emotions bubble up.

Step 3. Change the "I CAN'TS" to "I CHOOSE NOT TO." Actually, write them down so you can get them out in front of you. It should look like this:

I can't spend time with my kids. ——————> I choose not to spend time with my kids.

I can't return my emails. ————————> I choose not to return my emails.

Step 4. Notice what emotions or realizations come up when you realize these are all choices.

Step 5. What's the first smallest change or adjustment you can make (externally) that can help you feel less burdened and less trapped?

The Power of Belief

A few years ago, I worked with an attorney as a client. She ran her firm and felt like she was carrying a thousand-pound weight on her shoulders. It was her second session with me. In the first session, I worked with her to create little moments of calm throughout her day. I asked her to pause three times a day for three minutes at a time and practice one of the strategies I gave her. I knew she could do it because she was able to relax very well in my office. I also worked with her to put some very small systems in place that would help lift the heavy burden of being the leader of the firm off her shoulders.

She came back for the second session, and she was not only *even more* stressed out, but she was also frustrated!

I asked her what was going on, and she started telling me about all the problems that had come up since our first session. After she shared that with me, I knew she hadn't put any of the systems in place that we had talked about. This would have only taken her or her paralegal about an hour to do, and once it was set in place, it would have prevented all these problems from happening. I also knew she did not do any of the simple strategies I gave her. It became clear that she just wanted to come in and use our sessions as an outlet to complain.

When a client does this, it's actually detrimental to them, and it can prevent any results from happening. If this happens, I stop the client immediately and redirect the conversation. But this woman wasn't letting me get a word in edgewise.

I have a giant red flag in my office. As she was going on and on, I took out the red flag and waved it in front of her face, and shouted, "STOP!" She stopped dead in her tracks.

I said to her, "These were very simple things that you agreed to do. You didn't do them even though they would have taken minimal effort… and they would have helped you be less stressed."

I explained to her that I used these same systems and strategies along with many of my other clients who are business owners.

Then she screamed at the top of her lungs, "Well, Dan! Maybe *YOU* can own your business and be calm about it, and maybe your other clients can too… BUT I CAN'T!"

That right there showed me that she was missing two key components to make this work. She was missing belief, and she was missing worthiness. She didn't believe she could make any changes, and she didn't feel like she deserved to make the changes.

Henry Ford said, "Whether you think you can or think you can't, you're right!" I stand by that statement and would like to add "… until proven otherwise."

I told this woman, "You *really* believe you can't do this? Then what the f*ck are you doing here?"

I had to match her energy and meet her at her level to crack her shell. I use profanity very strategically, and talking to her like that finally got through to her.

Instead of working on reducing stress and plugging in systems *first*, we had to start with her feeling worthy enough and deserving, so she could be the person she needed to be to run her firm and actually enjoy doing it.

Before you make any changes, you have to make sure you believe you can, and you have to be willing to follow the necessary steps that it will require to get there.

Chapter 7:

Have To, Choose To, Get To

Do you ever look at your to-do list and get overwhelmed? Do you constantly say things like, "I have to do this" or "I have to get this done?" As a result, you get stressed out, start half-assing stuff, and say, "Well… that's good enough."

Guess what? This is a huge part of what's keeping you in a stressed-out and possibly underperforming state of mind.

In my *Break Free VIP* program, I talk a lot about the three levels of life:

Have to.
Choose to.
Get to.

Many people spend so much of their lives in the "have to" phase that they feel constantly pressured. So much of what they're doing seems a struggle because they feel everything in their life is in this constant state of "I have to do this, I have to do that."

The longer you stay in the "have to" mentality, the more stressed you'll be. Sure, we all have responsibilities to be functioning members of society. The more we live in the "have to" mentality, the less control we feel we have. This is why most high school students feel so much pressure, stress, and overwhelm. They're told they HAVE TO go to school, they HAVE TO participate in extracurricular activities, and HAVE TO get good grades if they want to get into a good college. Then they HAVE TO go to college (as a bare minimum) to get a good job, and then they HAVE TO go to work every day.

Jeepers, just thinking about that makes me stressed!

That's why it's important to have choices. In some of those "have to" obligations, there are some choices thrown in there. In school, you can (for the most part) choose your classes, you can choose what jobs you do, and you can choose your career path. Even though we have these choices, many people don't take advantage of them and fall back into the feeling of, "I have to do this."

After working with thousands of people and helping them resolve their stress and anxiety, some of our work is helping them form a plan to start working out of the "have to" mentality by helping them realize they have more choices. Then we can move into the phase everyone wants, but most people don't get there until later in life—if they ever do. It's a harsh and sad reality that some people don't get to the "get to" mentality.

"Get to" is when you can look at your life and feel like you're fulfilling and serving a purpose, and you really get to do more of what you want to do.

I'll give you an example from my life.

When I first began my career as a clinical hypnotist, I felt like I had to take on every client that called me, whether I wanted to or not. I felt an obligation to see as many people as possible. Even though I really loved what I did (and still do), I was taking on too many people because I *had to* make a living. I *had to* support myself. I was working hard (but not necessarily smart) because that's what I thought I had to do. That served me for a while. I made good money, and I got a lot of experience, but I was working my ass off.

I was seeing eight to ten clients a day, and three nights a week, I would also perform comedy shows. I would travel twenty weeks out of the year and speak and teach at professional conventions. I did all this because I felt I had to.

After about five years of doing this, it started to weigh down on me. I was getting not only burnt out but I was getting stressed out.

Because I do this work with my clients, I was able to see that I was getting burnt out and stressed, so that meant I should start finding other ways that allowed me to still enjoy what I was doing without getting overwhelmed.

I started cutting back on some of the things I told myself I had to do. I stopped taking on every client that called, and I stopped taking every travel opportunity that came my way.

I started charging more for my time, working less, making more, and working with people that I really enjoyed working with. The great thing was that my clients sensed that too. My family and friends also noticed. Instead of my friends, family, colleagues, and clients saying, "Wow, Dan, you look tired, you seem stressed, is everything okay?" they started saying things like, "Dan, you look and sound so much happier and healthier!"

I began focusing more on my physical health, and when I did, my business improved even more. I was feeling really fulfilled… then… it happened.

In 2021, my dad, who was my best friend and my biggest fan and support system got sick. He was diagnosed with stage four lung cancer. Just like he was my everything, I was his. I made the commitment to my dad, my family, and to myself to spend every moment I could with him.

I can say with an open heart and tears in my eyes that I *GOT TO* spend time with my dad during his final months on this earth. Was it sad? Yes. It was heartbreaking to see him slowly wither away. Was it stressful? At times. But guess what? The stress didn't matter. Not one effing bit because I got to be with my dad, and he got to be with me.

So look around. Notice some of the people around you who are stressed to the max, overwhelmed, and struggling to hold it together. I can almost guarantee that they live most of their life feeling like everything is a "have to" for them. You may not even have to look any further than in the mirror.

As you make some changes by using some of the strategies in this book, you'll discover that you have more choices than you realize. The more you move out of the *have to* mentality and more into the *choose to* and *get to* mentality, you'll find that you'll be bothered less and less by the things that used to seem like such a big deal.

I want to celebrate those wins with you. If you haven't already, scan the QR code below to hop, skip, and jump over to my free community, where I go live several times a month and post content that can really help you make breakthroughs. Just one breakthrough can change your entire trajectory and transform your life and your career. Are you ready for a breakthrough?

https://www.facebook.com/groups/anxietyreliefforp rofessionals

Chapter 8:

Living in the Land of Good Enough

Do you feel like you sometimes sabotage yourself and your success? Do you feel like you put self-imposed boundaries and limitations on yourself, and then you get upset with yourself when you can't break through that glass ceiling?

I see this with a lot of people that I work with. This is very common with business owners, entrepreneurs, and sales professionals. The biggest sources of stress can come from themselves and the limitations that they impose upon themselves.

The need for survival is one of our fundamental human needs, according to Maslow's hierarchy of needs. Some people fulfill that need and then just exist there because, from this place, they learn that their basic needs can be met by doing or maintaining the bare minimum. This is what I like to call *The Land of Good Enough.*

It's where everything is good enough right now. Things are going well—not great, but well enough.

This is where people get discouraged and wonder what the obstacle is.

For most, the obstacle is themselves. They have conditioned themselves to learn that where they are in life is just fine. They get comfortable with existing, so they stop pursuing activities that can make them thrive and grow, both personally and professionally.

This is where tasks pile up, people procrastinate or put things off, and this is where stress starts to creep in. But why does this happen? There are two main reasons.

The first is that the task that's being put off may not have enough reward attached to it to make it worthwhile doing. One of my former clients said, "Dan, I have so many ongoing projects in my house, and I haven't completed any of them! Why am I so lazy, and what do I do about it?"

One of the projects he was putting off was cleaning out his garage.

I asked him, "What will happen if you don't clean out your garage?"

He said, "Nothing."

"Right!" I replied, "Your wife won't leave you, your kids won't hate you, you won't make more money, etc. Not much will change other than your garage will be cleaner, and you'll have more space to put more stuff!"

I asked him a similar question. "What are the consequences if you don't clean your garage?"

He said, "Nothing, other than just feeling like a lazy loser, and that stresses me out."

His life was good enough, and there wasn't a good enough reward for cleaning his garage.

This left us with four options:

1. Don't clean your garage, and nothing changes.

2. Put bigger consequences in place if you don't clean your garage.

3. Put bigger rewards in place if you do clean your garage.

4. Outsource the cleaning of your garage and be satisfied with how they do it.

Our comfort level in the land of good enough is *just* pleasurable *enough* to outweigh the risk of doing activities that can make us thrive. This is where two big factors can get in the way… fear of success and fear of failure.

Why do we fear success?

It's not necessarily success we fear. We actually fear change. Most people fear the change that success can bring. Fear of failure has nothing to do with failure because if you fail at something, not much will change, but what we fear are the feelings of low self-worth we feel when we fail.

I'll provide more insight into how to solve these issues as we get further into this book.

Chapter 9:

Problems, Problems, Problems

There are two types of people:

1. People who see opportunities.

2. People who see problems.

The way you view a problem will determine your reaction or response to it. In this chapter, I'm going to teach you an exercise that can help you see opportunities even in challenging times.

You all know people like this...

You could win $10 million dollars, but there is always that one person who will say things like, "Ugh, you're going to owe so much in taxes, you'll hardly see any of that money. Also, just think about all the people who are going to come out of the woodwork and ask you for money."

People who think like that will rarely get out of that frame of thinking because they don't see anything wrong with it, and they aren't willing to change how they think.

Here is a way that you can shift your thinking when challenges or problems pop up.

What's Wrong with Me?

When people feel stressed or anxious, often it's easy to think that there is something wrong. Most people have a desperate need to figure out what the problem is in hopes that they can solve it. Well… not even solve it, but problems give a reason as to why something is going wrong.

One purpose of our subconscious mind is to find answers to questions that we ask ourselves, even if we have to create the answer. When we're feeling stressed out, we'll often ask ourselves, "What's wrong with me?"

What's even worse, when we see someone who is in freak-out mode or if we see them anxiously reacting to something, we often ask, "WHAT'S WRONG WITH YOU?"

I hear parents saying this to their children, partners saying it to their spouses, bosses saying it to their employees, doctors saying it to their patients, and even friends asking each other this debilitating question.

If you only take one lesson away from this book, let it be this...

Instead of asking, "WHAT'S WRONG WITH YOU/ME?" ask this... "What's going on with you/me?"

When you ask yourself what's wrong, your subconscious mind wants to find the answer, even if there is nothing wrong! Your mind will find something wrong or create it if it can't find something. It will put it in your awareness, and then, BOOM, there's another problem, and soon enough, your default way of thinking will be, *Something must be wrong.*

When you ask, "What's going on with me?" your mind will give you more insightful feedback and help you shift your way of thinking. This will be one small step that you can take to help you think like a problem solver instead of a problem creator.

Problem-Solving

Looking at problems and challenges in a different light is one way to avoid naturally falling into a stress response. Problem-solving is one of the greatest skills that anyone in the business world can master.

As Wayne Dyer said, "When you change the way you look at things, the things you look at change."

I have often had people message me on social media after seeing that I'm the Anxiety Relief Guy, and they say things like, "Nothing will help me. I've tried everything, and I'm too far beyond help."

I hate to say this… but they're right unless and until they change their belief system.

"If all you have is a hammer, then everything will look like a nail."—Maslow

The more we see problems, the more problems will occur. We get more of what we focus on.

When you're stuck in problematic thinking mode, it's difficult to solve that problem, and often we get stuck in the stress of the problem for longer than we need to be. There's a way to pull your focus out of problematic thinking and think more clearly by thinking outside the problem.

In the next chapter, I will outline some powerful ways to help you think about the problem differently, go into problem-solver mode, create solutions, and reduce your stress and worry so you can approach the problem with more of a calm and balanced state of mind.

Chapter 10:

Stress Buster and Problem Solver

Often, clients reach out to me when they're going through a personal or professional problem or challenge that they're struggling with, and it causes a great deal of stress for them. In this chapter, I'm going to share with you several strategies that I teach the people in my programs that help them see challenges differently, solve problems easier, and detach from the stress and worry that's often caused when dealing with these struggles.

Some of these strategies are very soothing and calming and may require you to close your eyes for a few minutes. Make sure you are in a place where you can dedicate a few minutes to practicing and applying these strategies. Once you learn them, it will become part of your second nature to use them. The more you use them, the better they will function, and the better they function, the less you will have to use them. Let's do this!

The Good in the Bad

As I mentioned before, we get more of what we focus on. When *life happens*, and we struggle to keep our sanity, we usually become more stressed because we magnify the problem by seeing *only* the problem. Something that can make us or break us when we are struggling with something is the questions that we ask ourselves. One way to instantly shift your way of thinking about the problem is by asking what I call *resolution questions*.

First, state what the problem is.

Next, ask yourself these questions:

> What is *one* positive thing about this problem?
> What *isn't* working or not the way it should be?
> What is *one* thing that can help make this better?
> What is the *first smallest step* I can take to make this better?
> What resource(s) do I have access to that can help solve this problem (or help me through this)?
> What is the *possible best* outcome?

By asking these resolution questions, you'll create more possibilities and begin strategizing with ways and resources that can lead to possible better outcomes.

Story Time: I get hired by many companies to teach workshops on various mindset and mental health topics. A few years ago, I was hired by a very well-known software company. They hired me to present my Anxiety Relief Power Hour. However, three days before I was about to give this presentation, I was notified by the human resources division that there was a massive problem in the company. One of the pieces of software they sold to a national security company had some major bugs, causing alarms to go off randomly in stores across the nation. Obviously, this resulted in many nasty phone calls and emails, many of which contained threats. HR asked if I could include some problem-solving strategies in my Anxiety Relief Power Hour. Of course, I happily obliged.

After I gave my opening remarks, I began talking about how thinking about the future and anticipating problems can lead to a great deal of stress and even fatigue. And how the current problems we are going through can lead to even more anxiety about those same problems happening again.

I started sharing more about the resolution questions.

There were about 200 people in the Zoom presentation, and when I asked, "What's one positive thing about this problem?" I didn't just get one answer. The chat was flooded with dozens and dozens of positives about the problem.

The responses ranged from things like, "We will have systems set in place to prevent this from happening again," to "I was starting to get bored with what I do here, and then this happened. At least I have something to do now."

We laughed at many of the responses, and as we continued through the resolution questions, we had several plans in place. In fact, more plans and solutions were created in twenty minutes than they would have been able to do in a week.

A key point here is to recognize that people will solve a problem in the amount of time you give them to solve it when they are aware of the right resources. The balance here is to make sure it's not creating unnecessary stress and pressure that will cause them to avoid doing it if expectations are unrealistic. If you give a team three weeks to solve a problem, it will take three weeks. If you give a team three days to solve the same problem, it will take three days.

The What If Paradox

The most stress-inducing questions are the "What if?" questions. Some people live so much in the "What if" that it's paralyzing and can keep them in a worried and anxious state of mind. When you ask yourself, "What if?" it can cause you to spiral downward and start worrying about things that will most likely never happen.

This is such a common theme with the people that are in my program that I have dedicated an entire process and session to help people overcome that "What if" worry loop. The worry that we get from the "What if" thoughts can be so strong that we'll start avoiding things if there's any thought of something going wrong.

Here's something to keep in mind that can help you if you have bad cases of the What ifs:

When we ask ourselves, "What if?" we often just stop there. We give up, or we spiral downward into fear and worry because we jump right to the worst-case scenarios. But keep this in mind. The "What if" is there for a reason. It's there to be aware of what the worse possible outcome could be so we can prepare for it. However, instead of preparing, most people just avoid it altogether.

When this happens, we entertain and even rehearse the worst-case scenario… but we skip step two. We forget to entertain the best-case scenario or any other good outcomes.

When you notice yourself "What if-ing" all over yourself, interrupt that pattern by contradicting each negative "What if" with a positive "What if." Here's how this worked with a previous client of mine:

Story Time: I was working with a woman who was in a high-level sales position. She had done very well with her career, closing some of her company's biggest accounts. Her customers loved her because she was personable and caring. The CEO noticed the successes she was making and offered her a promotion that would result in a $54,000.00 a year increase in her pay. I had worked with her previously just to help her increase her confidence and work through some family stress that she was experiencing. When she told me about this new promotion that she was offered, she told me that she might turn it down!

I asked her, "What's going on that makes you think you may turn it down?"

She started going down the "What if" path. "What if I'm not good enough and I lose everything? What if

I can't do the job they need me to do and I'm criticized? What if I can't handle the workload? What if I'm not respected?"

When she was finished, I asked her, "If you can come up with four negative 'What ifs,' certainly you can come up with four positive 'What ifs,' and probably even more than that. But let's give each positive 'What if' context. We have to put more energy into the good 'What ifs' than the negative ones."

She started forming some really thought-provoking success stories for herself. "What if I accept the job and I enjoy it even more than I am now? Then it won't seem like work to me, and I'll be even happier! What if I can do the job better than they expected, and I win awards and get the Hawaii end-of-the-year bonus? Then my family will have a free luxury vacation."

She continued down that good path for a while and became enthused and excited to accept the job.

So What? What Now?

Another powerful way to interrupt the "What if" pattern is to come up with the negative "What if" and then ask, "So what? How would I handle that?"

I call that the "So what, what now?" response. By responding in this way, you can create a more solution-oriented state of mind. Once you control the what-if thinking, it will happen less and less until it stops altogether.

If you'd like to see a video I recorded about this, you can go to: www.DanCandell.com/what-if

Chapter 11:

Switching Your Mindset from Stress to Success

Often, feeling stressed and overwhelmed can cause us to feel stuck or lost. When this happens, the natural inclination is to look outward, and we often become reactive to what's bothering us or stressing us out. Reacting to stress usually makes the situation worse. However, when you approach the challenge with a more calm state of mind, you can think more clearly, make decisions from a better headspace, and focus better, and even your overall mood and perspective will become more pleasant and optimistic.

The discipline of neuro-linguistic programming, or NLP, is a therapeutic modality that is based on modeling behavior and shifting your perspective to change your belief systems, habits, and internal programs. NLP is often combined with hypnosis to create a powerfully receptive state of mind so that you can easily make changes.

This chapter can be used as a reference guide to lead you through a powerful change process that takes five minutes or less.

Stepping into the Mentor Mindset

Often, when I work with professionals to help them change their minds about something or overcome challenges, stress, or anxiety, I ask if there is a coach, mentor, or someone they look up to. They usually start describing someone that they aspire to be like. This person has a mindset, abilities, and attributes that can be beneficial in stressful or high-pressure situations. Use this exercise by following the steps below, and you'll notice you'll be able to shift into a more powerful state of mind.

1. Think of a certain mindset, feeling, or attribute you'd like to have or have more of. This could be confidence, determination, pride, self-assurance, a calm demeanor, etc.

2. Think of a person who has what you want to acquire. This can be a mentor, a leader, a coach, or a fellow colleague. It can also be a celebrity. I have had some people say Oprah or Simon Cowell.

3. Close your eyes and take a few deep, slow breaths.

4. Imagine or think about the mentor or person you'd like to model.

5. Think about floating out of yourself and into them. See what they would see, hear what they would hear, and imagine responding as you believe they would respond.

6. Now, think of a situation you have been struggling with and think about how your mentor would handle it. What would they say? What course of action would they take?

7. Open your eyes, notice any insights you've received, and take action!

These techniques work well because your subconscious mind doesn't know the difference between that which is real and that which is vividly imagined. When you create these thought processes of thinking like your mentor, your subconscious mind thinks you're already thinking and responding that way.

Story Time: I was leading a client through this exercise, and I decided to make it interesting and let him have some fun with it. He needed help overcoming public speaking anxiety and feeling more confident. I guided him into a deeply receptive state using a hypnotic process so we could do these exercises in that headspace. When I asked him to float into someone he admired, his facial expressions changed, his voice changed, and he started speaking in a very clear, confident, and concise voice. It sounded very familiar. It sounded like I was talking to Barack Obama! When I asked who he floated into, sure enough, it was Barack Obama! This client was able to take and feel the confidence that Obama had.

Then I asked this client to float the mindset and ability to speak with calmness, confidence, and clarity into himself but leave Obama's voice back with Obama. The last thing I wanted was for this man to give a sales presentation and have people think he was modeling the former president.

Seeing Advice & Wisdom

There is a variation of the above technique that can also help when you need an extra boost. I call this the *mental pep talk*. It can literally help you with almost anything. I use this technique all the time whenever I need a mental kick in the pants or just some extra guidance. It's easy and quick, and you can do this pretty much anywhere. This can also help set your mind at ease if you're worried about something.

1. Think about a problem, challenge, or something in your life where you need some guidance.

2. Think about someone who could give you wisdom, guidance, advice, or insight.

3. Close your eyes and take a few long, slow, deep breaths.

4. Imagine or think about that person sitting in front of you telling you exactly what you need to hear.

5. Internalize their advice and notice any other insights you may receive.

6. Open your eyes and TAKE ACTION!

My clients and I have had so many profound experiences with this exercise, and it can just put your mind at ease. Many of my clients have gotten advice from parents who have passed, celebrities, and multimillionaires. I even had one client who received a pep talk from Morgan Freeman! Have fun with this.

Solving Problems from the Future

This is another good one that can help solve problems and give you clarity which can put your mind at ease and help with challenges. There is a principle that I call *precognition*. It's the ability to program into yourself a better sense of knowing. This is also a term from clairvoyance, which is when a person is in tune with their senses and has a feeling that they know what is going to happen. What if you could see ahead in the future when you've made it through the challenge you were dealing with and know that everything turned out fine? That would be reassuring, wouldn't it?

1. Become aware of something you have been struggling with or a problem that's been stressing you out.

2. Close your eyes and take a few long and slow deep breaths.

3. Imagine it's about one week after the problem that was stressing you out has been resolved, and you're having a conversation with a person close to you about how well it went and how it wasn't as bad as you thought.

4. What are some of the things you're saying? What has indicated that it wasn't that bad and that it wasn't worth it to get stressed out?

5. What are some ways you solved the problem that you're discussing with this person?

6. Open your eyes, and let yourself have a sense of peace and calm, knowing that things are more likely to go this way now.

The technique above helps us internalize the reality that "In the future, you'll be looking back on this, and it won't seem so important in the grand scheme of things." As cliché as it sounds, it's usually true.

Chapter 12:

Crushing Self-Doubt and Uncertainty

If you're feeling a little uncertain or questioning your ability, then it's time for a shift. Self-doubt is one of those sabotaging mentalities that prevents us from taking the necessary action that can lead to bigger and better things. This is also where we question if we're good enough. These are all thoughts that come from what I like to call The Itty Bitty Shitty Committee in your head. These thoughts and feelings can come from past experiences or projecting worries of "What if I'm not good enough" into the future.

Overcoming That Inner Critic

One of the main reasons why we doubt ourselves is because of our own inner self-talk, what other people have said to us, or thinking about what or how others will think.

Changing how you perceive that inner dialogue will change how it affects you. Follow these steps to crush the inner dialogue of self-doubt that's been sabotaging you.

1. Become aware of what you've been telling yourself or the internal dialogue that's been causing your insecurities.

2. Close your eyes for a moment.

3. Notice how that inner voice sounds to you. If it's from what someone else said, imagine they're saying it again to you.

4. Change the voice by making it sound like Mickey Mouse, and hear it like that.

5. Try changing it now to a sexy voice like the cartoon skunk Pepé Le Pew.

6. Try dulling the voice to a whisper.

7. If you can see the person in your mind, put Elmo's face over their face and change their voice to Elmo's.

Notice which one of these strategies or combinations works best for you to make that inner dialogue as ridiculous as possible.

Client Example: One of my clients is a financial advisor. I worked with him because he suffered from major imposter syndrome and self-doubt. He had been working with one firm for about two years. He got a better offer from a more prestigious firm but started questioning if he was good enough for that position.

I asked him what was going on that could have contributed to the self-doubt, and he opened up like a book. He shared with me that since he started working with his current firm two years ago, he was constantly being told that he wasn't working hard enough. He was told that he wasn't reaching out to enough leads, he wasn't fast enough, he wasn't direct enough, and he wasn't selling hard enough.

He said every time he thinks about accepting the better job offer, he keeps replaying in his head, "You're not good enough, you're not good enough, you're not good enough!" and it was stopping him from making the right decision.

I taught him one of my rapid relief techniques to change that internal dialogue, and here's what happened...

Every time he started replaying that internal dialogue, he used the technique I taught him. He accepted the job, and after he had been working there for about six weeks, everyone started complimenting him about how proactive he was, how fast he was getting things done, and how he was surpassing some of the senior advisors in the firm. He looked back at his previous position and realized the reason he was feeling stuck, stressed, and frustrated was because it was a toxic work environment and because they were giving him crap leads. Everyone else in the firm was getting high-quality warm leads, but they gave him only cold leads that were ten years younger than their typical clients.

Chapter 13:

Worry Buster

Worrying too much can lead to serious consequences like insomnia, difficulty concentrating, and even physical symptoms. Most people find themselves worrying about minor things that, in the long term, won't matter. Even though we know most of the things we are worrying about will never happen, worrying can still cause us to spiral downward and can lead to avoidance.

Business professionals can be especially vulnerable to this trap due to the intense pressure they might feel throughout their careers or businesses. To prevent worry from taking over, individuals must focus on the present moment by engaging in mindful activities such as meditating or deep breathing exercises. I'm going to share a powerful hypnotic and therapeutic strategy to help you manage those worries on a subconscious level. Ultimately, worriers who recognize their fears as something under their control are more likely to achieve success rather than just beating themselves up over nothing!

We all have different parts that compose who we are. It's important to know that every part of us has a positive underlying intention, even though some parts can limit us. Each person has an average of 137–157 parts. Some do their job from the background, and some come out in full force and sit in the control seat.

We all have an anxious part, a creative part, a worry part, a fun part, a sarcastic part, and so on. Here's how we can use these in relation to worry, stress, and anxiety:

When you're stressed or worried about something, first, become aware of those parts and acknowledge that they are *just* parts of you. They are *not* the whole of you.

Second, become aware of what their positive intention is. Usually, it's to keep you safe or prevent you from making reckless decisions that could embarrass you or put you in danger. Understand that this part literally thinks that if you don't listen to it or let it take control, then you'll make reckless decisions and do things that would put you in harm's way. It thinks that if you don't listen to it that you won't be *aware* of what you need to be aware of to stay safe. What we can do is have that anxious/stress/worry part team up with the awareness part so that the anxious part that's been harming you won't have to go into overdrive and control you anymore.

Quick Stress Relief Tip:

Here's how you can manage that part…

Doing this is a way that you can use to communicate directly with your subconscious mind:

1. Close your eyes.

2. Imagine that you can see that anxious part out in front of you. Sometimes it can help if you notice what it looks like. Some people say it looks like an animal, a shape, a person, or even a form of yourself.

3. Imagine you can talk to this part. What would you say to this part? Most people would say, "Leave me alone! I don't want you here anymore." But what we resist will persist. So let's take a different approach. Instead of resisting that part, let's give it another job.

4. Thank that part for trying to keep you safe, but let it know that it's been operating on information that's out of date, and now it's actually harming you. It may have helped

you in the past, but it's now doing its job *so* well that it isn't helping you anymore.

5. Tell that part to team up with the awareness part. Instead of being anxious all the time, you can be aware of what you need to do in order to start feeling better.

When you can communicate with this part of your mind and ask it to team up with awareness, you won't need the overly anxious part to work as hard, so it won't be holding you back anymore.

Now, make a mental movie or think about how your life will be different when the stress and anxious parts aren't in control anymore. Think about what will be different for you.

Chapter 14:

Turning Down Stress and Creating Better Outcomes

One of the reasons we get so stressed out and anxious is because of the pictures or thoughts about something we form in our minds. Think about it like this…

Imagine you get invited to a networking social. Imagine that there are going to be a bunch of desperate strangers there who don't know you, but they all want to try and sell you something. There is weird music blasting in the background and horrible stale finger foods that they are trying to pass off as gourmet hors d'oeuvre. You don't know anyone, so you feel out of place and just start to circle around, feeling lonely and looking at everyone else, making connections and engaging in conversations.

That seems horrible, doesn't it? I wouldn't go if that's how I was thinking about it. That's why most people avoid social functions or have social anxiety because these are the pictures they form in their heads.

Remember, our perceptions form our reality, and we get more of what we focus on. If that's how we thought that event would be, and we kept focusing on it from that perspective, of course we'd be miserable!

Let's try a slightly different scenario.

Imagine you get invited to a social networking event. You force yourself to go, but you're pleasantly surprised. When you walk in, some of your favorite music is playing in the background. As soon as you walk in, the staff pours you your favorite beverage. As you look around the room, you realize you know several people here, and you're excited to see them! You engage in conversations and catch up with them. As you're catching up, they introduce you to some people you will later benefit from knowing, and you introduce them to some people you know.

At the end of the social, a few of the people you met and really enjoyed talking to invite you to grab some dinner and cocktails at a place down the street... their treat. You go, and as you're leaving at the end of the night, you have a conversation with one of the people you met, and you're saying to them, "You know, I wasn't going to come, but I'm so glad I did! Let's do this again sometime soon!" As you drive home, you are truly happy that you went.

Which situation sounds better?

I'm going to go out on a limb and say the second situation sounds drastically better!

When we're avoiding something or feeling anxious or stressed, it's usually because we jump right into the worst-case scenario. Your subconscious mind doesn't know the difference between real and imagined, so by thinking about a worst-case scenario, you are more likely to make it happen or feel uncomfortable about it.

So how can we change your mind about this?

It's actually quite simple.

I used to do a lot of work with athletes. I would help them boost their confidence, eliminate performance anxiety, and teach them mental strategies that could help them perform well under pressure. There are actually a lot of congruencies between the mindset of a successful person in business and a successful athlete. You need many of the same attributes and mindsets to be successful in sports as you do in business.

There have been many studies done with athletes using visualization and mental rehearsal rather than just physical practice. Studies have shown that positive mental rehearsal is actually just as effective as actually practicing.

When we change the way we think and the images in our head, we change the outcome of a situation.

There's an effective way to do this. I use it with my clients, and it's called *the dimmer switch* matched with mental rehearsal.

Have you ever seen the movie *Inside Out*? It's the Pixar movie about how feelings, emotions, and core memories develop as we grow up. It's a very enlightening movie, and I have a lot of my clients watch it as homework.

In that movie, there's a control panel that controls the main character's feelings, emotions, and responses. When they adjust the intensity of an emotion on the control panel, there's a big screen where they can see how the main character responds to the adjustments they're making in her mind.

We can use this same premise to communicate with our subconscious mind.

Here are the exercises:

Quick Anxiety Relief Tip

1. Think of something that's been stressing you out.

2. Close your eyes, and take a few long, slow, deep breaths.

3. Imagine you can walk into your mind, and there's a control panel and a big movie screen.

4. Locate the section on the control panel where you find the controls responsible for stress and anxiety. They will be connected to dimmer switches like volume controls on a car radio. Turn them down like you were turning down a dimmer switch to something that's easier to manage.

5. Now locate the dimmer switches for calmness and confidence. Turn those dimmer switches up.

6. Project a mental movie on the screen of you now going through that situation, feeling calm and confident. Notice how you know you're feeling this way.

7. Float into the movie as if you were looking through your eyes, hearing through your ears,

and feeling and sensing through your mind and body.

8. Feel the adjustments you've made.

9. Open your eyes after you've experienced this for a few minutes.

This is a fun way to change how you feel about a situation. This works based on a cause-and-effect premise. When you turn something down, like anxiety, you should also turn something else up, like confidence or calmness. Each time you do this exercise, think about what you want to turn down and what you want to turn up.

You can also shortcut this by closing your eyes and making a mental movie of things going exactly how you want them to go and then floating into that movie as if you were experiencing what you were just creating on the screen. Repeat it three to five times, so lock it in place. When you float into it, you're trying it on like a new outfit.

Client Example: I was working with a motivational speaker, Dr. Jay. He traveled around the country and gave corporate keynotes at business conferences. However, one didn't go so well (it wasn't his fault), and he noticed anxiety building each time after that, right before he would get on stage. Then he noticed the anxiety building while he was traveling to the event, then when he booked the event. It was getting so bad he started to doubt himself and questioned if he should hang up his hat and call it quits as a motivational speaker.

I ran him through the exercise above and saw him for a few more follow-up sessions. His results were so phenomenal that he recorded a video testimonial that he allowed me to post on my YouTube channel.

All you have to do is use this technique and make it work for yourself. You'll notice a pretty rapid shift.

I recommend repeating this exercise once a day for five to seven days to make sure it takes hold in your mind and becomes a more permanent change.

Chapter 15:

Shifting Out of Stress and into Calm

In the following chapters, I'm going to outline mental, physical, and strategic ways that will help you not only reduce your stress in the moment but also help change how your mind and body respond to stress. These strategies will help you take the edge off, relax, and feel more inner peace. As a result of this, you'll be able to think more clearly and make more rational decisions.

Often when I work with people to help them decrease their stress and anxiety levels, they give me a list of everything that stresses them out and also all the problems they have. I'll give you the same advice I give to my clients. Let's not attempt to solve every problem right now. Let's just take this one step at a time and let ourselves experience calmness and peace. When you learn how to increase your levels of calm, something happens that I call the *carry-over effect*. This is when you make one small and sometimes subtle shift, and it carries over into many other areas of your life. I'll share a client example from an individual I worked with a few months ago.

Client Example: Sarah joined my group program for business professionals. She came into the program because she was feeling stressed and overwhelmed with the deadlines she had to meet. She owned a web design company and would get worried that she wasn't going to meet deadlines as they got closer. She'd stay up all night going over her to-do list in her head as she stared at the ceiling, trying to get to sleep. As a result of this, she'd wake up with no energy, and she'd drag throughout the day. When she got home, she'd be frustrated and have a short fuse with her husband and her family. The pressure and overwhelm she felt in her business carried over into her personal life too.

In the first two sessions of the group, she learned how to clear the stress, and she began practicing some of the techniques I'm going to share with you. As a result of letting herself feel more relaxed and calm, she was able to turn her mind off at night, which allowed her to sleep better. She was waking up with more energy and was able to focus more throughout the day. She was more productive and trusted herself to get things done. Because she was able to trust herself and take some of the pressure off, she was more pleasant at home with her family. The biggest thing she noticed was that she was smiling more and getting more done, and her daughter even said to her, "Mommy, you're not angry anymore!"

All this happened *just* by learning how to relax and feel more at peace. I'm confident that this same thing will happen for you too.

How to Use These Exercises

All these exercises are derived from hypnotic principles, NLP strategies, energy psychology, psychosensory therapy, and self-directed neuroplasticity.

These exercises will help you relax both mentally and physically, and they will help shift your thinking. They will literally *change your mind*.

The more you use these exercises, the better they will work and the less you'll have to use them.

To create a more natural calm, you should practice calm and resourcefulness more than you practice stress and anxiety. I gave an example earlier in the book of people who usually spend most of their lives repeating stress and anxiety. The more we repeat something, the easier and more natural it becomes, and the more frequently it happens. In order to switch off the stress and anxiety, we must practice calm responses more.

Build this into your day. Take three minutes three times a day (that's a total of nine minutes) and practice one or several of these techniques.

Most of these techniques will require you to close your eyes, so make sure you're not driving while you do them!

First, read through each technique from beginning to end and make sure you understand each one. Then practice the technique with your eyes closed. It's okay if you have to open your eyes every so often to make sure you have the steps down. Keep in mind that there's no right or wrong way. Just let each technique flow and make it work for you.

Chapter 16:

Rapid Relaxation Response

This exercise that I'm going to teach you is one that has gained me a lot of notoriety. I posted this technique on social media, and within two weeks, it got over 5 million views and tens of thousands of comments about how useful it is and how fast and effective it is. This only takes about sixty seconds to do, and you'll notice a powerful wave of calm go through your mind and body.

We can do this by creating heaviness in our bodies. When you make your body heavy, it causes all tension to leave your body, and your mind will stop racing.

1. Start off by sitting down and getting as comfortable as you can.

2. Drop your jaw as much as you can by slightly opening your mouth. This releases a lot of the tension that we hold in our jaw and facial muscles. Doing this also stimulates the vagus nerve and activates the parasympathetic nervous system, which helps you relax.

3. Close your eyes, and relax your eyelids to the point where they just won't work. Imagine they are glued closed or very heavy. Test this out by *trying* to open them. You'll notice that it's very difficult to open them as they *feel very heavy*. Even if you just have to pretend that your eyes are heavy, remember, your mind doesn't know that you are just pretending. When you do this, it tricks your mind into thinking that you're preparing your mind and body for sleep, so you start to feel more relaxed within about thirty seconds.

4. Take that same heaviness that's in your eyelids and bring it into your arms and legs. Make your arms and legs as heavy as possible, so it feels like they're loose and limp so they don't really want to move.

5. Drop your head down slightly while relaxing your neck and lowering your shoulders.

Stay in this position for a minute or two. Often, people will fall asleep while they're doing this, so you may want to set a three or five-minute alarm on your phone in case you do fall asleep.

Also, when you're this relaxed, your mind loses track of time. It may feel like thirty seconds, but chances are it will really be five to ten minutes that have passed.

You are learning restorative relaxation. You are giving your mind and body a mental break so you don't have a mental breakdown! Think of it as a mindset reset.

If you practice this three times a day for three minutes for about a week, you'll notice your stress levels naturally decrease, and you'll feel better and be able to perform at a better level.

Chapter 17:

Mental Relaxation

Most people who are in business or sales have thoughts that race through their minds constantly, and it can be exhausting. Sometimes we need to redirect our minds and our thoughts so we can mellow out and not feel so intense all the time. Practicing this mental relaxation technique before a call or a meeting will also help shift you into a more positive state.

This uses the power of thought and/or imagery. Our subconscious mind speaks in metaphors, symbols, and images. However, some people may have difficulty visualizing or making pictures in their minds, so just going through the thought process is equally as effective.

Before we dive too deep into this exercise, let's come up with a couple of things that can help guide you so you don't have to stress your mind out by trying to think of these things while you're doing the exercise.

Think of a place where you could imagine feeling at peace. Usually, this is a place in nature. Somewhere like a beach, a field, a meadow, a river, or even on a nature trail.

Next, think of a pleasant memory. It doesn't have to be the *perfect* one. Some people choose the birth of a child or a wedding. Some people choose a time when they got a promotion, closed a deal, or received a compliment. This memory can be warm and fuzzy or have a sense of pride and accomplishment connected to it. Some people choose a memory from childhood. It should be a memory that just feels good.

Sometimes people try to choose the perfect place or the perfect memory, but it's important to know that there's not always a *perfect* one. What first comes to mind is just fine. You can always change it when you repeat this exercise and see what comes up.

Here's the exercise:

1. Close your eyes and take a few long, slow, deep breaths. Exhale very slowly.

2. With your eyes closed, imagine, picture, or think about that calm place in nature. Think about the sights, the sounds, and even any smells or tastes that may be associated with it. Take a moment to really connect with this thought. Float into this image as if you're

becoming part of this peace just by thinking about it. Hold your mind here for about ten seconds.

3. Next, remember or recall that pleasant memory. Remember if you were indoors or outdoors, alone or with other people, and if it was daytime or nighttime. Give this memory as much content as you can. Remember where you were, who you were with, and what you were doing.

4. Float into this memory and recall the *feelings* that were connected to this memory. Become aware of these feelings, and let yourself experience these feelings again. Hold your mind here for as long as you need so you can feel a pleasant flow of these feelings, then open your eyes and smile.

When I teach this exercise to my clients, the first time they do it, many of them begin to tear up, and that's very common. These good feelings have become so foreign they bring tears to our eyes, but we can let ourselves feel this way again.

This exercise will help your mind shift into a more peaceful and optimistic state. It will give you rapid relief from stress and anxiety. The whole exercise, from beginning to end, only takes about one to two minutes and is a great way to reset your mind.

Chapter 18:

Floating Out of Stress and Anxiety

One of the main reasons we can feel so stressed out is that we feel so connected to the experience that's causing the stress. We also feel connected to the feelings. The more associated we are with stress, anxiety, and overwhelm, the more overbearing it can be.

This exercise will help you dissociate and disconnect from stress, anxiety, and the problems that may be causing it. It can also give you an outsider's perspective, which can give you more ways to solve a problem.

1. Sit down and get as comfortable as you can. Close your eyes when you are ready to begin the exercise.

2. Think about the thing that's been bothering you or all the stress and anxiety you've been feeling.

3. Imagine floating out of your body and looking down at yourself. Notice that from

here you can be completely disconnected from the stress, worry, and problems.

4. Float even higher, above the building you're in, above your town, above your state, above your country. Imagine you can float out of this world and just look down. Notice how small and insignificant things seem up here.

5. Float back down right above your body. Imagine making adjustments to your physical body that can create more calmness, relaxation, and solutions.

6. Imagine that you already have everything you need within you to feel more calm, confident, and at ease.

7. Float back into yourself and connect with the adjustment you've made.

8. Open your eyes.

A Variation on Dissociating from Stress and Anxiety

This variation can help you take more of an outsider's perspective and help you feel better about your current situation.

1. Get comfortable and close your eyes.

2. Think of the problem or challenge that's causing you to feel stressed.

3. Notice what picture or thoughts come to mind and float out of that image and see the back of your head.

4. Next, imagine floating around yourself and the situation and observing it from all angles.

5. Then drain all the colors from the image like it's a dull black-and-white old movie and push it as far away as possible.

6. Notice what's different and open your eyes.

The stronger things are, the more associated we are with them. If you want to weaken the intensity of any emotion or situation, shrink it down and push it far away.

If you want to make an emotion stronger, bring it closer and make the colors bright and vibrant.

This is all about shifting your perception. Remember, your perception becomes your reality. The more you can shift your perception, the more changes you can make, and the easier it is to make those changes.

Chapter 19:

Success Collage

When a challenge pops up, we see mainly that challenge. When we're stressed or anxious, we're not thinking about all the times when we felt calm or all the successes we've had. This can taint our perception of the world, and we become more negative and start to have a pessimistic outlook.

This exercise will help you shift out of that quickly and will help you feel more optimistic.

1. Think about what you want to leave behind you. It could be an energy, a realization, a bad year or experience, a bad memory, etc.

2. Notice the pictures, the sounds, and the self-talk that you've associated with this.

3. Take those pictures and push them far off into the distance. Notice any negative self-talk or sounds you've associated with this as well, and turn them down.

4. Now, create a SUCCESS COLLAGE of all the good things you have in your life. Imagine dozens of pictures of people you

like, successes, achievements, accomplishments you've made, good times you've had, or anything else you're grateful for.

5. Maybe replay some positive compliments you've received.

6. Fill your mind with positive sounds, experiences, memories, and images.

7. Next, in your mind, imagine a great big grid in front of you with nine squares on this grid.

8. And then fill eight of them with moments of success and happiness from your life—people, places, and moments. They could be accomplishments you've made, people you enjoy, experiences that fill your heart, or moments where you felt full and supported by life.

9. Leave the bottom middle square BLANK.

10. When you fill the other eight squares with all this BLISS and AWESOMENESS, and all the events, people, places, and times that make you feel good, add in the bottom middle square the image of you or that realization that makes you feel just yuck; however that feeling, thought, or image

manifests. It could be a color or dark energy, or it could be a feeling or reoccurring realization that doesn't fit you anymore.

11. Then look at all nine squares, and let your mind reconfigure how you feel. In the future, you'll only think back about that thing in the context of all the wonderful things you already have going on in your life.

Chapter 20:

Instant Shifts

The exercises in this chapter are some real next-level Harry Potter sh!t.

These strategies will help you shift your mood instantly. The great thing is you don't have to know how or why they work. Just know that this stuff DOES work. Experience it for yourself. Sometimes we overlook the effectiveness of something because of its simplicity. Approach these few strategies with an open mind, and I know you'll be impressed.

Eye Roll Shift

I remember in middle school, a teacher yelled at me, "Daniel! If you roll your eyes at me one more time, I'm putting you in detention."

Little did she know when I was younger, I had a minor case of Tourette's syndrome, and rolling my eyes was one of my ticks.

We are taught that rolling our eyes is a sign of disrespect. However, when you use it therapeutically and strategically, it works like magic.

Here's the entire exercise… ready?

1. When you're feeling stressed or upset, just roll your eyes up. That's all… just LOOK UP!

When you do this, it will shift your mood instantly.

If you really want to get next level here, then roll your eyes up, pick a focal point, and just hold your attention on that focal point. Imagine putting all your stress and anxiety into that little focal point and just leaving it there on that spot even after you're not looking at it anymore. When you roll your eyes up, you only need to do it for about ten seconds.

Think about it… we do this naturally when we try and stop ourselves from crying; we look up. If we need some more mental strength, we look up. This is something that is already programmed into us. Naturally, most of us just don't realize it.

Rapid Breath

"Just breathe" is one of the most irritating things you can tell someone who is stressed or anxious. This is especially annoying if it's said in a condescending tone. However, there is a mindset hack that instantly stops stress and panic responses. Ready? Here it is…

1. Take two RAPID breaths in through your nose, almost like you are forcefully sniffing something.

2. Exhale slowly through your nose like a long sigh.

3. For an extra added effect, make a pushing away gesture with your hand like you're pushing imaginary energy off to the side. This will send a signal to your mind that you're pushing that anxiety away from you.

This is another mechanism that's already built into us. Think about when you see someone cry. What do they do? They usually rapidly inhale and then exhale in an (emotionally painful) sigh.

See? Quick and easy.

Peripheral Vision

This is another fast and effective mind hack. This is one that they teach people in the military to help with focus, attention, and emotional intelligence.

When you're feeling any uncomfortable feeling, sensation, or emotion, follow these steps:

1. Focus on a spot slightly above eye level.

2. Slowly open your awareness by expanding your peripheral vision.

3. When you do this, you should have a blank look on your face as if you're daydreaming or in la-la land.

You only need to do this for about thirty seconds or so. This will help you reset your mindset so you can think clearly and create more of a calm and centered state.

Chapter 21:

A Deeper Approach

All these strategies that you learned in this book do one main thing. They help YOU take control. By taking control of the unnecessary stress and anxiety that have been controlling you, you'll start feeling better about yourself, your professional life will get better, and those changes will carry over into your personal life as well.

By practicing these techniques three times a day for three minutes—whether you need them or not at that moment—you'll be rewiring your mind and changing the way your mind and body interpret stressful situations.

The key is to practice these when you don't need them and in times when you're not that stressed out so you can master them and use them when you feel you do need them. It's extremely difficult to learn something new or focus when you're stressed or anxious, so instead, learn these and practice them when you're not in that scattered headspace.

Consider these resources and tools that you can use anytime and anywhere.

It doesn't matter how long you've been stressed or anxious. It's never too late for you to gain control and start practicing and repeating calm responses more than you practice and repeat stressful ones.

Often, people who have read my books and applied these principles still want or may need a deeper and more personalized approach. This is something I offer for people who may want to work more closely with me in my program.

In my Break Free VIP program, I use many mental, emotional, and subconscious clearing techniques that work on a neurological level. They help clear the underlying emotional core of stress and anxiety. I also guide you through deep healing processes and clear outdated limiting beliefs. This is where we really break those old patterns of behavior.

If you haven't yet, head over to the resource guide for this book at www.StressReductionBook.com/Resources, and you can also join my free Facebook community, *Anxiety Relief for Business Professionals*, where I go live just about every week and post exclusive content in that group. You'll also see case studies from clients that have gone through my program.

If you would like to join one of my programs and get a deeper approach to help you break free from stress, worry, anxiety, and overwhelm, you can find the details of my programs at www.DanCandell.com

Be well, do good, and be true to who you are.

Dan Candell
Your Anxiety Relief Guy
Board-Certified Hypnotist

Printed in Great Britain
by Amazon

25927087R00076